DIRK NOWITZKI

BY MARTY GITLIN

Printed in the United States of America,
North Mankato, Minnesota
092011
012012

 THIS BOOK CONTAINS AT LEAST 10% RECYCLED MATERIALS.

Editor: Chrös McDougall
Copy Editor: Anna Comstock
Series Design: Craig Hinton
Cover and Interior Production: Kazuko Collins

Photo Credits: Wilfredo Lee/AP Images, cover, 1; Donna McWilliam/AP Images, 4, 19; Holger Sauer/Getty Images, 7; Gero Breloer/AP Images, 9; David Zalubowski/AP Images, 10; Elaine Thompson/AP Images, 13; Eric Gay/AP Images, 15, 16, 24; Tony Gutierrez/AP images, 21; Lynne Sladky/AP Images, 22; David J. Phillip/AP Images, 27; Tom DiPace/AP Images, 29

Library of Congress Cataloging-in-Publication Data
Gitlin, Marty.
  Dirk Nowitzki : NBA champion / by Marty Gitlin.
    p. cm. — (Playmakers)
  Includes bibliographical references and index.
  ISBN 978-1-61783-292-5
  1. Nowitzki, Dirk, 1978—Juvenile literature. 2. Basketball players—United States—Biography—Juvenile literature. I. Title.
  GV884.N69 G57 2012
  796.323092—dc23
  [B]
                              2011039417

TABLE OF CONTENTS

Dirk Nowitzki

CHAPTER 1

WÜRZBURG TO DALLAS

irk Nowitzki was born in Würzburg, West Germany, on June 19, 1978. His mother Helga had played professional basketball. And his father Jorg-Werner was a successful team handball player. But Dirk preferred tennis. He wanted to be just like West German tennis star Boris Becker. Dirk even copied Becker's haircut.

But it soon became clear that Dirk's future was in basketball. He was already very tall by age 12.

Dirk Nowitzki holds the Dallas Mavericks' career record for points scored.

A doctor said that Dirk would grow to become a seven-footer. So Dirk decided to take up basketball. He felt very comfortable on the court. After all, he did not stand out so much for being tall there. A lot of other players were tall too.

Dirk also found some new heroes. They were the members of the Dream Team. That was the nickname of the 1992 US Olympic men's basketball team. Some of the most famous basketball players ever were on that team. Among them were Larry Bird, Magic Johnson, and Michael Jordan. The 14-year-old Dirk watched them win the gold medal on television. He decided he wanted to be a star basketball player just like them.

Basketball was a growing sport in Germany. But Dirk dreamed of playing in the National Basketball Association (NBA). That is where Bird, Johnson, and Jordan played. And the league is in the United States and Canada. Dirk worked very hard to get there. And he had the help of West German Olympic basketball player Holger Geschwindner.

Geschwindner coached and trained Dirk. He made sure the young basketball player was fit. The coach also focused on shooting and passing. Those are skills that some big men

Dirk played for the Würzburg professional basketball team in Germany prior to joining the NBA.

struggle with. However, those skills later helped Dirk become a star in the NBA. Dirk and his coach focused on more than just basketball, though. Geschwindner also helped Dirk to be a well-rounded person. He encouraged the youngster to play the saxophone. Dirk also enjoyed reading.

Geschwindner saw that Dirk had great basketball skills. So he paid a visit to Dirk's parents. They had no idea their son was so talented. But they soon found out. Dirk joined the Würzburg professional team as a 17-year-old. He became a starter in his second season. And in his third season, he averaged 28.2 points per game. Dirk's effort helped his team move to the first division. It also caught the attention of NBA scouts.

More and more NBA teams were looking in Europe for players. Dirk was invited to the Nike Hoop Summit game in San Antonio, Texas. That game features top young basketball players. Many scouts for college and NBA teams came to watch. Dirk put on a show. He scored 33 points and grabbed 14 rebounds. One person who was impressed was Bird. He was now the Indiana Pacers' coach.

Many European teams wanted Dirk to play for them. Some offered him millions of dollars. But Dirk had his mind set. He wanted to play in the NBA. Dirk got his wish. The NBA Draft is

Dirk still spends his summer vacations in Würzburg. Some of his friends have even postponed their weddings until the summer so Dirk can attend. Dirk also enjoys time with his family. He especially looks forward to his mother's stuffed cabbage.

Dirk received Germany's highest sports award, the *Silberne Lorbeerblatt*, in 2011.

held each year for teams to select players new to the league. Dirk had to serve in the military for one year in Germany. Then he was free to go.

The Milwaukee Bucks selected him ninth in the 1998 draft. But the Bucks immediately traded him to the Dallas Mavericks. And that is where he stayed through the 2010–11 season.

Dirk Nowitzki

CHAPTER 2

AN NBA ALL-STAR

It did not take long for Dirk Nowitzki to make an impact in the NBA. He became the Mavericks' starting power forward by his second season. He led the team in rebounds that year. And only one Mavericks player scored more points than he did.

The team improved greatly too. Dallas had gone 19–31 in 1998–99. That season was shortened because NBA players and owners had disagreements. The next

Nowitzki became the Mavericks' starting power forward in 2000–01. He started every game that season.

year, in 1999–2000, the Mavericks went 40–42. That was their 10th straight losing season. But it would be their last for a while. Nowitzki and the Mavericks had not had another losing season after that through 2010–11.

Nowitzki helped turn the team into winners. Guards Steve Nash and Michael Finley played big roles too. The Mavericks won 53 games in 2000–01. That was good enough to make it to the playoffs. Dallas had not been in the playoffs since 1989–90. The Mavericks won 57 games the next year. Then they won a team-record 60 games in 2002–03.

Nowitzki played just 16 of the 53 minutes in his first NBA game. He missed all five of his shots, he had no rebounds, and Dallas lost in overtime. But two nights later, he scored 16 points. He also led the Mavericks with 12 rebounds. And they won!

Nowitzki had already reached great success. He made his first All-Star team in 2002. That was his first of 10 straight seasons in the All-Star Game through 2011. But fans often judge players by their success in the playoffs. Nowitzki had led

Nowitzki, *center*, Steve Nash, *left*, and Michael Finley, *right*, led the Mavericks to the NBA playoffs in 2001.

the Mavericks to the second round in 2001 and 2002. And he had led them to the conference finals in 2003. But fans wanted more. They were upset when the Mavericks lost in the first round in 2004. They were also bothered when they lost in the second round of the 2005 playoffs.

Nowitzki himself played well in the playoffs. He averaged at least 23.4 points and 8.1 rebounds per game during those

Nowitzki still plays for the German national basketball team. He has not had much success, though. Germany did not qualify for the 2000 or 2004 Olympic Games. And it finished 10th in 2008. Nowitzki was picked to carry the flag at the 2008 opening ceremony.

seasons. Those numbers meant little without a championship, though.

One of Nowitzki's off-court goals was to help children in need. So he created his own foundation. It helped children in many ways. Nowitzki worked to raise money for kids with kidney disease. He provided funds to help poor children buy school supplies. He also helped homeless youth get food, shelter, clothing, and playground equipment.

The 2006 season was exciting for the Mavericks. The team again won 60 games. And this time, the Mavericks won in the playoffs. They reached the NBA Finals for the first time in team history. Nowitzki led the charge. He even scored 50 points in one game during the conference finals.

The Mavericks faced the Miami Heat in the Finals. And the Mavericks continued their strong play. Dallas won the first two games at home. It also took a lead in the third game. But then

Nowitzki led his team against the Miami Heat in the 2006 NBA Finals, but the Mavericks fell short of a title.

the Mavericks caved in. Miami came back to win Game 3. The Heat then won the next three games and the championship.

Nowitzki was upset. He was the Mavericks' star. The team looked to him for leadership. But he had shot poorly during the series. There was no doubt that Nowitzki was a top NBA player. But some people began wondering if he would ever lead a team to an NBA championship.

Dirk Nowitzki

CHAPTER 3

PLAYOFF FRUSTRATIONS

irk Nowitzki had turned the Mavericks into winners. He even led them to the 2006 NBA Finals. Many experts believed he was among the best players in the league. And Nowitzki continued to play at a high level in the season that followed.

Nowitzki averaged 21.8 points per game in 2000–01. He has averaged at least that many points every season through 2010–11. He also averaged

Nowitzki looks for a teammate to pass to during the 2008 playoffs.

between 7.0 and 9.9 rebounds per game during that time. And Nowitzki was a trusted scorer. He made at least 46 percent of his shots. Nowitzki has also made approximately 88 percent of his free throws in his career. And he ranks among the top 25 players in NBA history in points scored.

Still, Nowitzki struggled to gain respect. Fans knew he was good. But they did not think he was great. They compared him to San Antonio Spurs power forward Tim Duncan. But Duncan had led his team to four NBA titles from 1999 to 2007.

A CHARITABLE CHAP

The NBA presented Nowitzki the Community Assist Award in 2004 and 2007. The league also donated $5,000 to his foundation.

The 2006–07 season was especially frustrating for Nowitzki. The regular season went well. He led the Mavericks to a 67–15 record. That was the best in the Western Conference. It was also the best record in Mavericks history. And the NBA named Nowitzki its Most Valuable Player (MVP). Many favored the team

Nowitzki won the NBA MVP Award in 2006–07, but the Mavericks' playoff struggles continued.

to return to the NBA Finals. But the dream season ended soon after the playoffs began.

Dallas played the Golden State Warriors in the first round. The Warriors had barely made the playoffs. But they had won all three games against Dallas in the regular season. The Mavericks' struggles against the Warriors continued in the playoffs. They lost the series four games to two. It was an upsetting loss. Dallas became only the third top-seeded team to lose in the first round.

Nowitzki struggled during the series. He scored just eight points in the final game. And he missed all but two of his 13 shots. The team leader's performance was similar to the team's. The Mavericks lost the game by 25 points.

The loss held up many people's beliefs. Nowitzki was a very good player. But he was not a championship player. Nobody was more upset than Nowitzki, though. He knew his talents. And he knew that he had not played to his skill level in the playoffs.

Nowitzki continued to play at a high level during the following regular seasons. And he continued to play at a high level in the playoffs too. But the Mavericks struggled. They lost in the first round of the 2008 and 2010 playoffs. And they lost in the second round in 2009. Many people thought the Mavericks' best days were behind them. Nowitzki was 31 years old in 2009–10. Were his best days behind him, as well?

Through 2010–11, Nowitzki has made more three-point shots than any other player in Mavericks history.

Dirk Nowitzki

CHAPTER 4

FINALLY A CHAMPION

Dirk Nowitzki was not the NBA's flashiest player. But he worked hard. He scored lots of points. And he was a popular player. But, he had never won a championship. That standing only seemed to grow as his career went on.

It did not matter that Nowitzki had led the Mavericks to the playoffs every year since 2000. Nor did it matter that he averaged nearly 26 points and more than 10 rebounds per game in the playoffs.

Few people expected the Mavericks to be an NBA title contender going into the 2010–11 season.

The Mavericks rallied around Nowitzki to lead them to an NBA title in 2010–11.

The critics still believed Nowitzki could not win the big game. They said he was not a great team leader. As such, few people put the Mavericks in the championship race before the 2010–11 season.

There was little reason to. The Los Angeles Lakers had won the previous two NBA titles. And they were again the favorites. Many people favored the Miami Heat too. They added stars

LeBron James and Chris Bosh that off-season. And they already had a star in Dwyane Wade.

Most people thought the Mavericks would again be a playoff team. But they did not expect much more. After all, that is what always happened. But something different took place. The Mavericks surrounded Nowitzki with talented veterans. Center Tyson Chandler helped Nowitzki under the basket. Forward Shawn Marion could do many things well like Nowitzki. And guards Jason Terry and Jason Kidd directed the offense. Only Nowitzki and Terry remained from the 2006 NBA Finals team.

All of those veterans had one thing in common. None of them had won an NBA title. They knew this might be their last shot. And they knew Nowitzki had to be the player to lead them there.

Dallas finished the season with a 57–25 record. That was the third-best record in the conference. Nowitzki indeed led the way. He scored a team-high 23 points per game. With help from Chandler and Marion, Nowitzki did not have to play such a big role in rebounding.

A TRUE SUPERSTAR

Nowitzki won the NBA's MVP Award in 2007. He was also named first team All-NBA in 2005, 2006, 2007, and 2009.

Fans started to get excited about the Mavericks as the playoffs began. The team had experienced players. And those players were driven to prove people wrong. That was very clear in the second round. The Mavericks swept the Lakers in four games. Nowitzki was the star. He led the team in points in three of the four games. And he twice led the team in rebounds.

More people began believing in Nowitzki. He led the Mavericks past the Oklahoma City Thunder in the conference finals. Dallas lost just one game in the series. And Nowitzki led the team in scoring in all five games. Marion was tied for the lead in two of the games. Now Nowitzki just had to do the same thing in the NBA Finals. And he would have to do it against a familiar opponent, the Miami Heat.

Many people were rooting for Nowitzki. They liked the teamwork he and his teammates showed. And many also disliked Miami. Fans were upset that James left his hometown

Nowitzki grabs a rebound during Game 2 of the 2011 NBA Finals. The Mavericks beat the Miami Heat 95–93.

Cleveland Cavaliers to join the Heat. They wanted to see Nowitzki win the title more than James.

The teams split the first four games. Nowitzki then took over in Game 5. The game was close with three minutes to play. Then Nowitzki swooped to the basket for a dunk. That basket gave Dallas the lead. And the Mavericks never let it go. Nowitzki scored a game-high 29 points in the win.

Nowitzki returned to Würzburg to celebrate his 2011 NBA title. The city threw a huge party in his honor. Right after the game, thousands of townspeople had poured into the street to celebrate the Mavericks' victory even though it was 3 AM in Germany.

The Mavericks could seal the victory in Game 6. But the loud fans in Miami did not make that easy. Nowitzki missed 11 of his first 12 shots. And Dallas blew an early lead. People began to wonder if they were right all along about Nowitzki. He seemed to be off his game when he was needed the most.

But then he exploded for 18 points in the second half. Ten of those points came in the fourth quarter. Nowitzki and the Mavericks took control and won. After 13 years in the league, Nowitzki was a champion. He was also named NBA Finals MVP.

Nowitzki knew he had quieted his critics. He had proven once and for all that he was indeed a champion.

Nowitzki and his Dallas Mavericks teammates celebrate their first NBA championship in 2011.

FUN FACTS AND QUOTES

- "He's like a lot of European players in that he doesn't like contact. He has a lot of work to do, but he's smart and he can handle the ball. He has the kind of potential that leaves you curious." —Mavericks assistant coach Donnie Nelson after watching 19-year-old Dirk Nowitzki play. Some inside the NBA have claimed that European players do not thrive in a more physical game.

- West German Olympic basketball player Holger Geschwindner first watched Nowitzki play basketball in 1994. Nowitzki was just 15 years old. Still, the coach was motivated to approach the youngster. He said Nowitzki had very good basketball instincts. The Olympian became Nowitzki's coach soon after.

- People often questioned Nowitzki's ability to win big games. But not only did he win the 2011 NBA Finals, he did it while he was hurt. Nowitzki tore a tendon in his left middle finger in Game 1. But he decided to continue playing. And he played well enough to win the title and the MVP Award.

- Championship-winning athletes often make extra money endorsing other products. Nowitzki is not one of them. He considers himself only a basketball player. He does not embrace the business side of his profession. He does not even have an agent. Nowitzki negotiates his own contracts with the team.

WEB LINKS

To learn more about Dirk Nowitzki, visit ABDO Publishing Company online at **www.abdopublishing.com**. Web sites about Nowitzki are featured on our Book Links page. These links are routinely monitored and updated to provide the most current information available.

GLOSSARY

charity
Money given or work done to help people in need.

draft
An annual event in which the top amateur basketball players are selected by NBA teams.

dunk
The act of slamming a basketball through the hoop.

foundation
A trust that gives money and other support to people in need.

rebound
To catch the ball after a missed shot.

scholarship
Financial assistance awarded to students to help them pay for school. Top athletes earn scholarships to represent a college through its sports teams.

scouts
People who watch basketball players to determine which ones their team should pursue.

veteran
Experienced players who have been in the league for a long time.

INDEX

FURTHER RESOURCES

Ballard, Chris. *The Art of a Beautiful Game: The Thinking Fan's Tour of the NBA*.
New York: Simon & Schuster, 2009.

Frager, Ray. *Dallas Mavericks*. Edina, MN: ABDO Publishing Co., 2012.

Ladewski, Paul. *Megastars 2010*. New York: Scholastic, 2010.